The Chinese Zodiac

Aaron Howe

DEDICATION

This book is for those on a never-ending
quest for knowledge.

CONTENTS

ACKNOWLEDGMENTS

This book contains information that I'm bringing forth from my research along with my own personal beliefs. Thank you.

Aaron Howe

1 INTRODUCTION

Hello and welcome to *The Chinese Zodiac by Aaron Howe.* I'm your guide, Aaron Howe. In this book, I will be going over one of my favorite topics, The Chinese Zodiac. This is a quick and easy guide for those of you that are new to this topic, or for those that like to keep things simple. Before we begin, I'd like to introduce myself a little better. As I said before, my name is Aaron. I'm a Spiritualist and a firm believer in The Chinese Zodiac.

I have written several books, fiction and non-fiction, on a wide variety of topics. My goal is to share my knowledge on this topic with you, and help you use it in your everyday life. All I ask of you is to keep an open mind. Alright, now we can begin. I want to start by giving you a quick history lesson on The Chinese Zodiac. Its origins are apparent by the title, I know. I want to tell you about the when, where, and why.

The selection and order of the animals that influence people's lives originated in the Han Dynasty (202BCE - 220AD). It was based upon each animal's character and living habits. The division was mostly related to the number 12. One ji (which is the cycle) equals 12 years. One year has 12 months. One day has 12-time periods called shi chen (modern day hours). Ancient people of many cultures observe that there are 12 full moons within one year.

So, its origin is associated with astrology, in its own way. The difference is that the alignment of the planets has nothing to do with you or your sign. Each animal sign is usually related with an earthly branch, so the animal years were called Zi Rat, Chou Ox, Yin Tiger, Mao Rabbit, Chen Dragon, Si Snake, Wu Horse, Wei Sheep, Shen Monkey, You Rooster, Xu Dog and Hai Pig. It's a lot simpler than it sounds. Try not to overthink it. The following chart shows a quick breakdown of the animal signs and where they fit in on the wheel.

The Chinese Zodiac Animal Wheel

As I said before, it really is quite simple. It's a lot less complicated than Greek Astrology, which relies on many variables that are constantly changing. After examining the wheel above, do you know what your sign is? Before we get into all of that, let's take a step back into history and further examine the origins of The Chinese Zodiac.

It is believed that the 12-lunar month calendar of China was created during the 27th century BCE under Emperor Huang Ti. This was just the beginning, though. By the time of the Shang Dynasty, between the 16th and 11th centuries BCE, a complex mathematical system had been developed with a greater understanding of astrology and the universe as a whole.

It was this better understanding of time itself, which led to the creation of the 12-month cycle and eventually to The Chinese Zodiac. No one knows for sure when this happened though. Or how, for that matter. There are a lot of different theories, but the true origins of the animals chosen and who choose then is still a mystery. The 12 signs of The Chinese Zodiac are, in order: Rat, Ox, Tiger, Rabbit, Dragon, Snake, Horse, Sheep, Monkey, Rooster, Dog, and Pig.

Of course, your animal sign isn't the only factor in The Chinese Zodiac. There is also a system of elements attached to the calendar. Not to mention how the Yin and Yang fit in. Let's start with the five elements. All of the Chinese zodiac signs pass through them. The elements are Fire, Wood, Water, Earth, and

Metal. Everyone and everything must interact with these Elements. They are all a part of life itself according to the teachings of The Chinese Zodiac.

Each element is associated with one of the planets in our solar system. Fire is paired with Mars, Wood is paired with Jupiter, Water is paired with Mercury, Earth is paired with Saturn, and Metal is paired with Venus. This is where the similarities to Greek Astrology come into play. Greek Astrology is very heavy on the relationship to the planets in our solar system. With The Chinese Zodiac, the astrology is mostly related to the elements.

Each of these Chinese elements has a connection to another. They each have a beneficial, destructive, and a hostile relationship to the other elements. The beneficial relationships are as follows: Water generates Wood, Wood generates Fire, Fire generates Earth, Earth generates Metal, and Metal generates Water. Now for the destructive relationships. They are as follows: Water puts out Fire, Fire melts Metal, Metal cuts Wood, Wood breaks Earth, Earth swallows Water, and Rock beats Scissors… I might have made up that last one. Finally, the hostile relationships are as follows: Water hates Fire, Fire hates Metal, Metal hates Wood, Wood hates Earth, and Earth hates Water. Keep all of that in mind when looking to make new friends or finding a mate.

Each of these elements has their own set of characteristics that affect the animal signs. As each of the elements pass through the animal signs, these characteristics modify the animal signs. This makes changes to the normal characteristics of that sign. There are 60 different combinations in the Chinese zodiac.

The concept of Yin and Yang also affect the five Chinese elements, as I said earlier. This means that there is a Yin Fire and a Yang Fire. The way it is set up in the Chinese zodiac is that Yin falls in odd numbered years and Yang falls in even numbered years. Thankfully, that part is simple enough. Before we go into detail on the Yin and Yang, here are the elements explained further.

Chinese Fire Element

Those born with the Fire element love adventure and excitement. They have dynamic personalities and are excellent leaders. They are competitive and may become restless if not challenged in life. Fire elements tend to have a rather magnetic attraction. They don't like to be secluded away from others. Excluding them is one of the worst things you can do. They prefer to form strong bonds with their loved ones and are very protective.

Fire is confident and sure of itself. They like to explore new things and ideas. They are brilliant minds with warm hearts. They can be very decisive and dramatic at times. They may be aggressive about achieving the things they want in life. They overcome most obstacles in their way. Fire people are gifted speakers and can be very clever.

They can be hypersensitive at times as well, so be careful not to offend them. The Fire element may become selfish and inconsiderate if they are bored with what they are doing. They become impatient when they are thwarted in their ambitions. Even though they are good at overcoming obstacles, Fire people may get hung up if they start to rush things. If you befriend a Fire person, keep this in mind so that things will move smoothly. They will reward your tact with their signature warmness.

The Fire element is the South and represents the season of summer. Fire's obvious color is red. It is associated with the heart. They should stay away from too much heat and emotion or they may just combust!

Chinese Wood Element

Those born with the Wood element are generous and kind. They strictly adhere to their sense of ethical behavior. They are natural born explorers. Their powers of persuasion are very strong, so be warned. Wood people are often artists in whatever they do. They are diligent and committed to their work. They like to be busy and believe that hard work is good for you. They are very confident.

They have a deep appreciation of what they have. They don't bother themselves with things they don't feel they can attain. They usually have many different interests. They are loyal friends and can always be counted on. They do not indulge in selfish behavior, normally. They love working on a team and don't like to be alone. They are very compassionate and tactful with others.

Wood may tend to take on more than they can handle and become overwhelmed. One thing they need to work on is learning their own limits. Find a subtle way to point it out to them, since they won't like being told that directly. They may become overly dependent on others. Wood tends to be passive and inhibited. It is easy for them to lose themselves in the crowd.

The Element of Wood is the East. It is associated with the season of spring. Green represents the Wood element. Keep track of your liver and gall bladder if this is your element.

Chinese Water Element

Those born with the Element of Water can be charming and sensitive as well as compassionate. Known for their flexibility, they tend to *go with the flow.* They are often intelligent and creative people. They have a great imagination and are not afraid to use it! Sometimes to the annoyance of others around them. They make excellent philosophers and are deep thinkers. They often have more than one profession at a time.

Water has good people skills and can be subtly persuasive. They are talented communicators and make great diplomats. They are intuitive and can find things that elude others. They are very organized in everything they do. They have the gift of noticing the special talents of others and making them feel good about their abilities.

Water can also be secretive and deceptive. They don't like to share their secrets with others, big or small. They have great skills of manipulation. Water tends to try to find the easiest way out of any situation. They may be too passive and malleable to the whims of others. They need to learn to stand on their own two feet and follow their own path. They should avoid places heavy with water. It will weigh them down.

Water element is the North. It is associated with the season of winter. Water's color is black, and it is associated with the lungs, skeleton and excretory system. Mind your health when it comes to those things. Water people are more likely to break bones than the other elements. They also tend to be clumsier, so be careful!

Chinese Earth Element

Those born in the Earth element are patient and reliable. This element has a high sense of duty towards the people they are close to. They are ambitious and idealistic. They approach problems in a logical and methodical manner. They follow their intuition and have strong deductive talents. They are the moral compass by which they judge the world. They are very ethical and disciplined.

Earth people make great police officers and judges. They have the ability to use their resources wisely. Their conservative nature helps them most of the time, but can hinder them when a more open-minded approach is necessary. They also make good planners or administrators. They are usually wise in all financial issues, so they can be trusted with money. They have a talent for keeping things in their proper perspective. Their steadiness and reliability will impress all those around them.

They are disciplined and tend to not show their emotions. Earth people can be hard to read at times. They want to be important and loved. It would do them well to become a bit more adventurous in life. They tend to stay in familiar territory. They are usually respected and admired. The Earth sign may be considered stubborn or rigid most of the time. They may be controlling or only interested in their own abilities to gain. They may end up questioning their own instincts and distrusting their wisdom when feeling down. They have a fear of the unknown that can be very strong.

Earth is the Center. It is the changing of the seasons. Earth's color is yellow, and it is associated with the digestive system, especially the stomach and spleen. Earth people should watch for ulcers and acid reflux. They would do well to stay away from wetlands and moisture. A dry place like the desert is a great place for an Earth sign to live.

Chinese Metal Element

Those born with the Metal Element are tenacious and self-reliant. They like to be nomadic and can be loaners. They like to enjoy themselves but do care about and respect others, despite the way it may appear. They are usually pretty reserved, but when pushed they can be very forceful and unyielding. Metal signs tend to be introverts.

Metal likes to live in an orderly fashion. They keep things as simple as possible. They prefer a balanced environment and like things to be clean. Metal is confidant and determined in life. This can set them apart from all the others except for Fire. Metal and Fire have the same drive. When a Metal person knows what it seeks, they pursue it unflinchingly.

Obstacles and setbacks do not bother them. They are natural problem solvers. They don't mind solitude and prefer to be left alone. They tend to be virtuous, and their inner strength of character is well known. Metal creates their own success and sets out to attain it with a single purpose. Metal can be very impulsive. They have a liking for luxury and power.

They tend to be greedy and have a knack for making money. They can be unreasonable and stubborn. Metal people may become set in their ways and not open to change. They are demanding when in charge and expect all those around them to meet their high expectations. Metal is the West. It is associated with the season of autumn. Metal's color is white. In the body, Metal is associated with the respiratory system and the lungs in particular. Metal people tend to have breathing related issues like asthma. If you are a metal person, stay away from smoking.

Yin & Yang

What is the Yin and Yang? That is a question with many answers. Although you may hear Yang energy described as *positive* and Yin energy as *negative* there is a lot more to it than that. Both the Yin and Yang are necessary to the balance of life. The Yin and

Yang are both good and evil, light and dark, yes and no, and a whole lot more.

Everyone and everything is made up of both Yin and Yang. Each animal of the zodiac is distinguished be the Yin or Yang. This means that each animal leans towards either the Yin or Yang. As an example, Tigers are Yang and Snakes are Yin. This doesn't inherently mean that some signs are good, and others are evil. It is merely which end of the balance they lean towards. Knowing whether your sign is more Yin or Yang will help you to understand its characteristics better.

A relationship between a Yin and Yang sign is complementary. These two will balance each other out. Whereas two Yin or two Yang personalities might have more issues and be less compatible. In any relationship, it all comes down to how the animal signs align with each other. That is the key fact and is more important than the Yin and Yang.

Let's keep are focus on the animal signs. As I said before, there are 12 animal signs of The Chinese Zodiac. Rat, Ox, Tiger, Rabbit, Dragon, Snake, Horse, Goat, Monkey, Rooster, Dog, and Pig. I have put together a chart to break things down in more detail. This will show you which signs are Yin and Yang. It will also show the corresponding element to your birth year. Consult the chart below (or the one in Chapter 14) to find your sign.

First find your birth year and then you will see your animal sign and element. Once you have figured out your animal and element, you can read the appropriate sections to discover more about yourself. It's that simple! Just use the provided chart.

The Chinese Zodiac Table:

Birth Year	Sign	Element	Principle	Birth Year	Sign	Element	Principle
Feb. 06 1932 – Jan. 25 1933	Monkey	Water	Yang	Feb. 13 1965 – Jan. 20 1966	Snake	Wood	Yin
Jan. 26 1933 – Feb. 13 1934	Rooster	Water	Yin	Jan. 21 1966 – Feb. 08 1967	Horse	Fire	Yang
Feb. 14 1934 – Feb. 03 1935	Dog	Wood	Yang	Feb. 09 1967 – Jan. 29 1968	Sheep	Fire	Yin
Feb. 04 1935 – Jan 23 1936	Pig	Wood	Yin	Jan. 30 1968 – Feb. 16 1969	Monkey	Earth	Yang
Jan. 24 1936 – Feb. 10 1937	Rat	Fire	Yang	Feb. 17 1969 – Feb. 05 1970	Rooster	Earth	Yin
Feb. 11 1937 – Jan. 30 1938	Ox	Fire	Yin	Feb. 06 1970 – Jan. 26 1971	Dog	Metal	Yang
Jan. 31 1938 – Feb. 18 1939	Tiger	Earth	Yang	Jan. 27 1971 – Feb. 14 1972	Pig	Metal	Yin
Feb. 19 1939 – Feb. 07 1940	Rabbit	Earth	Yin	Feb. 15 1972 – Feb. 02 1973	Rat	Water	Yang
Feb. 08 1940 – Jan. 26 1941	Dragon	Metal	Yang	Feb. 03 1973 – Jan. 22 1974	Ox	Water	Yin
Jan. 27 1941 – Feb. 14 1942	Snake	Metal	Yin	Jan. 23 1974 – Feb. 10 1975	Tiger	Wood	Yang
Feb. 15 1942 – Feb. 04 1943	Horse	Water	Yang	Feb. 11 1975 – Jan. 30 1976	Rabbit	Wood	Yin
Feb. 05 1943 – Jan. 04 1944	Sheep	Water	Yin	Jan. 31 1976 – Feb. 17 1977	Dragon	Fire	Yang
Jan. 05 1944 – Feb. 12 1945	Monkey	Wood	Yang	Feb. 18 1977 – Feb. 06 1978	Snake	Fire	Yin
Feb. 13 1945 – Feb. 01 1946	Rooster	Wood	Yin	Feb. 07 1978 – Jan. 27 1979	Horse	Earth	Yang
Feb. 02 1946 – Jan. 21 1947	Dog	Fire	Ying	Jan. 28 1979 – Feb. 15 1980	Sheep	Earth	Yin
Jan. 22 1947 – Feb. 09 1948	Pig	Fire	Yin	Feb. 16 1980 – Feb. 04 1981	Monkey	Metal	Yang
Feb. 10 1948 – Jan. 28 1949	Rat	Earth	Yang	Feb. 05 1981 Jan. 24 1982	Rooster	Metal	Yin
Jan. 29 1949 – Feb. 16 1950	Ox	Earth	Yin	Jan. 25 1982 – Feb. 12 1983	Dog	Water	Yang
Feb. 17 1950 – Feb. 05 1951	Tiger	Metal	Yang	Feb. 13 1983 – Feb. 01 1984	Pig	Water	Yin
Feb. 06 1951 – Jan. 25 1952	Rabbit	Metal	Yin	Feb. 02 1984 – Feb. 19 1985	Rat	Wood	Yang
Jan. 26 1952 – Feb. 13 1953	Dragon	Water	Yang	Feb. 20 1985 – Feb. 08 1986	Ox	Wood	Yin
Feb. 14 1953 – Feb. 02 1954	Snake	Water	Yin	Feb. 09 1986 – Jan. 28 1987	Tiger	Fire	Yang
Feb. 03 1954 – Jan. 23 1955	Horse	Wood	Yang	Jan. 29 1987 – Feb. 16 1988	Rabbit	Fire	Yin
Jan. 24 1955 – Feb. 11 1956	Sheep	Wood	Yin	Feb. 17 1988 – Feb. 02 1989	Dragon	Earth	Yang
Feb. 12 1956 – Jan. 30 1957	Monkey	Fire	Yang	Feb. 03 1989 – Jan. 26 1990	Snake	Earth	Yin
Jan. 31 1957 – Feb. 17 1958	Rooster	Fire	Yin	Jan. 27 1990 – Feb. 14 1991	Horse	Metal	Yang
Feb. 18 1958 – Feb. 07 1959	Dog	Earth	Yang	Feb. 15 1991 – Feb. 03 1992	Sheep	Metal	Yin
Feb. 08 1959 – Jan. 27 1960	Pig	Earth	Yin	Feb. 04 1992 – Jan. 22 1993	Monkey	Water	Yang
Jan. 28 1960 – Feb. 14 1961	Rat	Metal	Yang	Jan. 23 1993 – Feb. 09 1994	Rooster	Water	Yin
Feb. 15 1961 – Feb. 04 1962	Ox	Metal	Yin	Feb. 10 1994 – Jan. 10 1995	Dog	Wood	Yang
Feb. 05 1962 – Jan. 24 1963	Tiger	Water	Yang	Jan. 11 1995 – Jan. 18 1996	Pig	Wood	Yin
Jan. 25 1963 – Feb. 12 1964	Rabbit	Water	Yin	Jan. 19 1996 – Feb. 06 1997	Rat	Fire	Yang
Feb. 13 1964 – Feb. 12 1965	Dragon	Wood	Yang	Feb. 07 1997 – Jan. 01 1998	Ox	Fire	Yin

2 THE RAT (YANG)

The Rat sign is the first animal in The Chinese Zodiac. They tend to be charming, but overly aggressive. Rats can also be very expressive and talkative. They are natural party animals *(no pun intended)* that love a good time. The Rat can be quiet at times, but it's very rare.

Rat people make many acquaintances, but very few friends. The friends they do keep, they cherish. Rat people tend to keep their feelings to themselves and don't share much with those around them. Rats can grow bitter with life and become mean, narrow-minded, and stuck-up. Rat people are normally pretty honest, if asked a direct question. However, they can bend the truth if it will benefit them in the long run.

Rat people can become very successful in life if they can overcome their general discontent for life. They also insist on living in the present and very rarely think of the future. Rats are quick witted and can be sarcastic often. They can also get a lot done in a short amount of time when they make the effort.

Rats are usually pretty confident and have good instincts. They are usually very stubborn and want to live by their own rules. Rat people will have trouble being around someone who likes to take charge. Rat signs are perfectionist by nature and are very hard to work with. They are good in business and politics. They are very bad with money. Rats tend to spend it the moment it comes in.

Rats rarely lend out money, and when they do, expect them to be all over you for it back. They have very little trust in people and can be greedy with money. The Rat is not a romantic. They may think they are, but they're definitely not. They are sensual and loving, though. Rat people are not easy to date, but if you can break down their walls, they are well worth the wait. Rats are very loyal and devoted to the one they are with.

Compatibility

Rat signs are most compatible with Dragon, Monkey, and Ox. They are least compatible with Horse, Rabbit, and Goat.

3 THE OX (YIN)

The Ox is the second sign of The Chinese Zodiac. Oxen are hard-working and very black and white. To them, there is no middle ground. There is no neutral. Everything is either good or bad. Oxen are very linear people. Don't expect them to be open-minded. They can be extremely judgmental of others.

Ox people feel that they are very important and that everyone around them should aspire to be more like them. Ox people are not very social. They tend to hate large crowds and socializing, in general. Ox signs can be very impulsive and fearsome when angered. They tend to overreact to even the smallest of things. Ox people have great memories and will be sure to use this to their advantage during an argument.

They have no quarrels with bringing up past issues even if previously resolved. Ox's can be very petty when arguing and have no tact. So be prepared to have your feelings hurt with their low blows. Ox signs would do good to work on their social interactions. It is harder for them to be respectful compared to other signs of the zodiac. A lot of this stems from their inflated sense of self. With good effort, Ox signs can overcome this aspect of their personality.

It is getting them to realize this about themselves that is the true challenge. Oxen aren't good at self-analyzing. The Ox is very observant and intelligent. They do well in jobs that require good hand eye coordination. Oxen are extremely stubborn and dogmatic.

They rarely apologize for anything no matter how much evidence is stacked up against them.

They are usually disappointed with all those around them. This is because they feel like no one is smart enough to understand them. Ox's can be very arrogant. They are usually oblivious that they are acting that way and will get defensive if you point it out. Despite all of their negative traits, Ox people can be patient, caring, and can make good friends.

Some very influential and powerful people have been born under the sign of the Ox. This includes: Adolf Hitler, Aristotle, Barack Obama, Gerald Ford, Johann Sebastian Bach, Margaret Thatcher, Napoleon, Princess Diana, Richard Nixon, Robert Kennedy, Saddam Hussein, and Walt Disney.

Compatibility

Ox signs are most compatible with Rat, Rooster, and Snake. They are least compatible with Tiger, Horse, and Dragon.

4 THE TIGER (YANG)

The Tiger is the third sign of The Chinese Zodiac. Tiger signs are natural born leaders. Tiger is the animal that represents authority. They are proud and will exert their leadership wherever they may go. Whether they mean to or not. It is simply in their blood. Forceful and aggressive, they are usually in the lead and it is difficult to deny them their rights.

It is of no coincidence that many of the world's most famous leaders are born under the Tiger sign. Some examples are of this are: Sun Yat-sen, Ho Chi Minh, Jiang Zemin, Karl Marx, Dwight D. Eisenhower, Charles De Gaulle, Queen Elizabeth II, and Marco Polo.

The Tiger has a great deal of self-confidence and no setbacks can stop them from achieving their goals. They leap over all obstacles in their way. Tigers tend to be noble and fearless. They are usually respected for their courage, even by those working against them. They set high realistic goals and work hard to achieve them steadily and consistently. Tigers are only happy when they see everything settled and completed.

Tigers are daring fighters and will stand to the bitter end for something they think is right. They are unpredictable and always tense. Tigers are usually in a hurry. They don't like to waste any time and lead fast-paced lives. They like to get things done. Tigers can be tempestuous yet calm. Tiger signs are hard to resist.

Their natural air of authority confers a certain prestige on them. Tigers like to be obeyed and not the other way around. Tiger signs usually choose to work alone. They don't like being held back. When a Tiger undertakes a job, it will be done with enthusiasm and efficiency. They can come off selfish at times, but it's usually over little things. In reality, they are very generous people.

The Tiger loves to be the center of attention and they look for approval from peers and family. They do like their alone time, though. It would be wise to learn when a Tiger wants to be left undisturbed. The astute and quick-thinking Tiger knows how to take advantage of situations. The Tiger will rise to power and positions, where he will excel even further in what he sets out to accomplish.

A humanitarian, the Tiger will fight for noble ideals, especially when it concerns something close to their hearts. They will fight for a loved one or their honor. They are definitely not the type to be oppressed and pushed around and are known to be rebellious. Tigers are always ready to put up a good fight for the rights of others. They tend to do what they feel is right despite any rules or regulations against their cause.

Tigers radiate enthusiasm and have a tremendous amount of energy. These qualities enhance their ability to command and persuade others. As they are always eager to please, they are well known for their lively and charming personalities. Tigers easily endear people around them by just being themselves.

Tigers are very good at making money, but are not directly interested in it. They like simple things. This carefree attitude in regard to money seems to attract more and more to them. Just when a Tiger is about to go broke, money seems to come their way. Tigers are adventurous and highly competitive. The Tiger loves challenges. He is always active and out trying new things. Looking for the next big challenge.

The Tiger does this mostly to prove that he can accomplish it as successfully as the last challenge. Tigers are constantly on the lookout for the next mountain to climb or the next milestone to make. They love to take chances and tempt fate. Sometimes, a little too often. Most of the time, Tigers emerge even stronger than before and won't hesitate to tell you all about it!

The Tiger believes in the "all or nothing" or "do or die" approach. They really do feel that way. They will risk their life for certain achievements. Some may view this as reckless, but Tigers are very calculated and know what is at stake. As Tigers are very assertive, once they set sight on something they want, it's very hard to stop them. Not motivated by money or power, they are not easily influenced to take sides or sway from their original goals and have incredible focus in what they set out to do.

Tigers usually think and act fast, and hence can be regarded as abrupt, hasty or impulsive. Their direct and outspoken character may not be welcomed by everyone. As I mentioned earlier, Tigers want to get things done fast. This makes them want to work alone, even when they should have help. If you really want to help a Tiger, ask them if you can join them. This is a much better method than implying that they NEED the help. Tiger signs can be quite self-centered and like to do things their own way.

They often don't like putting value on

others' opinions believing theirs is the best way. The Tiger will be very disturbed and even depressed if they fail at a task, or feel unproductive in their daily lives and at work. This sadness can last for a day or two, or until they can feel accomplished again. As success-oriented as they are, they also don't take criticism well, especially from loved ones. They feel attacked, hurt, and even betrayed by this.

The Tiger likes to dominate and be in charge and has little tolerance for error or incompetence. Tigers can be very unforgiving at times He will even revolt against authority and superiors to prove a point. At their worst, if Tigers feel they are not respected or being put down, they can become hostile and plot revenge. Tigers firmly believe in "an eye for an eye". Especially if they are betrayed or the other party has been malicious to them. They might even take hasty action without analyzing the situation which could result in quite a storm!

On the flip side, Tigers will rarely hold a grudge. They will most likely blow off some steam and move on with their life. They have too much going on to worry about the opinions and actions of sheep! Overall, Tigers are very balanced. They are mostly happy in life and are associated with the Yang. Tigers are very loving. They can be very intense about it, which some find overwhelming.

They are also very territorial and possessive. If you are friends with a Tiger, they'll expect you to always take their side. The Tiger is so adorable that, often you will. As lovers, Tigers are passionate and romantic. The Tiger's real challenge is to grasp the idea of moderation. With all of that being said, Tigers are normally pretty easy to get along with for almost anyone.

Compatibility

The Tiger sign is most compatible with Dog, Horse, and Dragon. They are least compatible with Snake, Ox, and Goat.

5 THE RABBIT (YIN)

The Rabbit is the fourth sign of The Chinese Zodiac. Rabbit people, like their animal counterpart, are very delicate and fragile. Rabbit people are usually very nice and sweet people. They tend to be very popular and have a large circle of friends. They are rarely ignored and always make good company.

Rabbits keep their home clean and artistic. They have good taste and like to be praised for it. Rabbits dress well and will rarely be seen in rags. Rabbits have expensive taste. Sometimes this taste will exceed their budget. They don't care though. They would rather keep up the appearance of wealth, even if that means a secret struggle to survive. Rabbits are always concerned with how others view them.

Rabbit people hate challenges. They are very insecure and conservative. They don't like anything beyond what they are already use to. They can also be very pessimistic. Rabbit people are relatively calm. It is pretty hard to get them riled up. They hate to argue and like peace and quiet. Rabbit people can be extremely sensitive and cry very easily.

Rabbits are easily moved by a compelling story. They are gullible and timid. Rabbits tend to fall for even the simplest of tricks. Rabbit people take a longer than most to make decisions. They like to view things from all angles and will need extra time to evaluate any situation. Rabbits don't make good leaders. They don't like hurting people and lack what it takes to make tough decisions. This makes them great assistants for people.

Rabbits tend to live very normal and mundane lives. They are good listeners and make great partners in a relationship. They are very romantic and faithful. Rabbits are usually attractive and always have many options when it comes to dating. Male Rabbits tend to be pickier than their female counterparts. Female Rabbits tend to be very self-absorbed. If they can work past these traits, Rabbits can have very successful marriages.

Compatibility

The Rabbit is most compatible with Pig, Goat, and Dragon. They are least compatible with Rooster, Rat, and Horse.

6 THE DRAGON (YANG)

The Dragon is the symbol of the Chinese emperors. This is mainly because the Dragon is a born leader. Chinese parents adore their Dragon children. In fact, Dragon years have the highest birth rates in China. Dragon people are real go-getters and they are good at keeping the ball rolling towards their goal. They can be feisty and extremely lucky.

Dragons are admired by most. They feed off of this and parade around like monarchs. They feel in charge of every situation and that their authority is indisputable. Dragons are very inflexible. They truly believe they are born perfect and that nothing about them needs to be changed. This lack of self-awareness will drive certain people away from them relatively easy.

Dragons are highly aggressive and have a strong determination to get their way. This can make them very dangerous people. They will do whatever they deem necessary to get what they want with no regard for those in their way. Dragons have an unhealthy lust for power. They have a fear of growing old and weak. Most Dragons live short and chaotic lives.

Dragons are irritable and stubborn. They have big mouths and will often throw insults around with no concern for the feelings of others. They do, however, give good advice. As long as what they are advising you on doesn't interfere with their own agenda. Just be careful on how you speak to Dragons, as they lose their temper easily. Dragons have huge egos and want you to worship them.

When a Dragon enters a room, they will start running their loud mouth in order to get everyone to look up at them. It is an utter waste of time to try and advise a Dragon on anything. They believe that they already have all of the answers. You are just a peasant and they are the king or queen. They can be very tyrannical and love to give orders. They hate taking them, though. They will even throw a temper tantrum if anyone tries to command them.

Unlike the Tiger and Ox who impose their wills seriously and firmly, the Dragon will treat everyone around them as if they were slaves and that they must obey or be punished. Dragons are very stuck-up. They care more about wealth and prestige than those around them. The Dragon is usually very intelligent and successful in most careers.

Compatibility

The Dragon is most compatible with Rat, Pig, and Monkey. They are least compatible with Dog, Rooster, or another Dragon.

7 THE SNAKE (YIN)

The Snake slithers in at the sixth position in The Chinese Zodiac. Snakes have a stigma around them in modern culture that is unjustified. They are viewed as the evil seducers that are looking to harm us, but this couldn't be farther from the truth. Snake people are naturally very charming and magnetic.

Snakes tend to be popular and like being the center of attention. They refuse to be ignored and love to entertain. Snakes can be outspoken, but this is usually by accident. They don't like to cause trouble and tend to have very good manners. Snakes signs are very friendly and like to work hard. They will fulfill any project they set out to do, no matter how hard it may become.

Snakes tend to attract a lot of suitors towards them, but tend to be uninterested in their possible mates. You will really have to *wow* a Snake person to get their attention. Snake people make good leaders. They can make decisions swiftly and firmly. Snakes are very intellectual and make good philosophers. They love to have civil debates on a wide variety of topics.

Be careful when first meeting a Snake, first impressions are everything to them. It will be very hard to recover from a faux pas in the beginning. Being the sixth sign, Snakes possess a sixth sense. If they have a bad feeling about someone, their opinion of the person will never change. Sadly, Snakes usually misjudge most people. They need to learn to give people second chances.

Snake people can be very tight with money. When they do lend it out, be prepared for them to be on your case about it. Furthermore, even after paid back, Snakes tend to hold the fact that they helped you over your head. Snakes tend to exaggerate their accomplishments to all of those around them. One thing they can brag about is money. Snakes tend to attract a lot of money to themselves. They might spend a lot of it, but they are good at bringing more in to balance things out.

Snakes can be a bit lazy. They should find a career they like and stick with it. As far as love goes, male Snakes can be very charming. Female snakes are a bit different. They are usually very beautiful and successful, but may be a bit picky and self-absorbed. Snakes are very jealous and possessive in love. They have a very delicate ego, so tread lightly with them.

Compatibility

Snakes are most compatible with Rooster, Ox, and Dragon. They are least compatible with Pig, Rabbit, or another Snake.

8 THE HORSE (YANG)

The Horse is one of the most active and energetic signs of The Chinese Zodiac. Horse people are usually in great shape and make exceptional athletes. They also tend to have a lot of sex-appeal. They are the life of the party and frequent concerts, movies, and sporting events.

Horse people tend to be very quick-witted and are able to steal the words right out of your mouth. The Horse sign is gifted in many different ways. They may appear to be very intelligent, but in reality, they are more cunning. This is no surprise to them. They are aware of their strengths and weaknesses. In fact, Horse signs are more self-aware than most of the other animals. This keeps them grounded and humble.

Despite all of their strengths, many Horse people lack confidence. There is no real reason for this. It is good for them to be around people that will help to lift them up. Horse people always like to be on the move. They really enjoy travelling and will want to live in many different places.

Horses are ambitious and rebellious. They may not outwardly show this, but they are definitely ready to burst in the right moment. Horse signs are inpatient and hot-headed. They have trouble fitting in and making friends. Horses can be selfish at times, but nothing too extreme. They aren't the hardest working, but they can get the job done.

Horses are great with money and investments. They know how to make it, how to save it, how to spend it, and how to get it all back. Horses are very generous and don't have a greedy bone in their body. This can also be a weakness, if they allow the wrong kind of people into their life. Horses will give up everything for love. They really will! When a Horse loves someone, it runs deep.

The Horse sign can be a bit confusing at times. There are a lot of aspects to them that contradict others. Horses are proud and arrogant yet humbled and modest. Horses need to feel independent, but also that they are a part of something important. They need to be loved, and thirst for intimacy.

Be careful on how you approach this with them since they feel pressured easily. They long and the short of it is, Horses depend on only themselves to achieve what they want in life. They are loving and interesting people that can make great mates. Horses won't tolerate liars or people that they feel are toxic to them. Horse signs will lose interest in someone very quickly if they're bad for them. Don't worry, Horses are not overly judgmental.

If they have a problem with you, they are likely to talk to you about it ahead of time. In general, Horse people are open-minded and will give you your fair chance. Furthermore, Horses aren't afraid of change. They are surprisingly open to it. They may even become enthusiastic about certain changes they can make in their lives. Especially if it is to please a partner. Horses should look for a partner with similar interest and good communication skills.

The Tiger is the best match for them. The two have adventurous and positive personalities. They both share a need for excitement. The Horse Tiger relationship will be characterized by loyalty and respect. Two traits that both signs place a lot of value in. They also benefit from working together. Whether the Horse chooses a Tiger or not, they need to find someone they truly feel right with or it won't work in the long run.

Compatibility

The Horse sign is most compatible with Tiger, Dog, and Goat. They are least compatible with Rat, Monkey, and Ox.

9 THE GOAT (YIN)

The Goat sign radiates elegance and charm. Creativity and artistic finesse comes naturally to people born under this sign. They are delicate people much like the Rabbit. Goats have good manners and are generally pretty polite. Goats can be insecure and need to feel loved and protected all of the time. They can attract friends very easily.

Goats usually get themselves into bad situations. They hate conflict and will usually flee from even the smallest of battles. They are bad at decision-making and will all out refuse to choose a side of an argument if pressured. Goats can be over-anxious and pessimistic. They are often unhappy with outcomes that they know are good and beneficial. The saying *misery loves company* applies to them greatly.

Goats are lazy and care little for work or love. They want to be taken care of and often marry for money. Goats blow in the direction the wind goes, so don't expect much loyalty from them. On the upside, Goat people can be very romantic. They are sensitive and sweet, as well. Be wary of their bossy nature. This isn't because they want to be in charge or feel authority. They are bossy because they want to be taken care of and pampered.

Compatibility

Goat signs are most compatible with Pig, Rabbit, and Horse. They are least compatible with Ox, Rat, and another Goat.

10 THE MONKEY (YANG)

The Monkey is a fun-loving, cheerful, and energetic sign. Monkeys can take any mundane situation and turn it into a lively party. The Monkey will be at the center of the party, as well. They are quite humorous too! They are creative and talented in everything they do. The Monkey is clever and cunning.

They could even be called mischievous at times. Not necessarily in a bad way, though. They can be very playful people. They might play a practical joke on you. Although, Monkey people can be deceptive when they want to be. They are honest people, most of the time, but don't have many inhibitions about lying. When dealing with a Monkey, keep in mind that they may not be how they outwardly seem.

Monkey signs are very diplomatic and have great people skills. They are great about hiding how they really feel about people. They could hate the ground you walk on, but still smile at you and be extra polite. Some may see this as being insincere, but to them, it's just being smart. One thing Monkeys don't hide is their emotions. They want everyone to know how they are feeling whether it be happy or sad.

The Monkey is a natural problem-solver. They are very knowledgeable. They do well in careers that require someone to clean up the previous persons mess. Monkeys excel in business and politics. They are very reliable and take good care of their family, friends, and lovers.

Monkeys are great persuaders. Too good, in fact. They sometime tend to trick themselves into believing that they are doing what's right, even when they aren't. This can be their downfall. Some Monkey signs can be self-centered and opportunistic. That isn't necessarily a bad thing, though. This helps them in business, greatly.

Monkeys are extremely indifferent in most situations. They usually aren't opinionated and tend to be carefree. They do have firm beliefs on certain things, but overall, they don't care what anyone else does as long as they are left alone. More people should adopt this trait from the Monkey. It's always good to keep at least one Monkey in your circle of friends.

Monkeys have amazing luck and tend to attract money to themselves. They are more likely to be well-known or famous than some of the other signs. Their charm gets them a long way with most people. They are hard to dislike. In friendship, Monkeys are loyal and devoted. They don't make the best lovers if you are looking for the long term. They are passionate, but unlikely to stick around. They are more likely to cheat then other signs.

Monkeys fall in love easily, but get bored fast. Once the boredom sets in, they are on the hunt for their new love. Sometimes, without breaking off their current one! This isn't to say that all Monkeys have infidelity issues, just be careful. One minute you are with your passionate Monkey, and the next... Your Monkey is sitting on someone else's branch playing with their banana!

Compatibility

The Monkey is the most compatible with Rat, Dragon, and Pig. They are least compatible with Horse, Snake, and Rabbit.

11 THE ROOSTER (YIN)

The Rooster is one of the most observant signs of The Chinese Zodiac. Their observations are usually spot-on, and they are great at reading people. Like the Snake, they have a sixth sense which they rely on often. Roosters are very straightforward.

There is no mystery to them. How they appear really is how they are. This separates them from other signs like the Monkey. The Rooster has a big ego that needs to be stroked constantly. The Rooster will let you know if he/she approves of your admiration. Roosters tend to dress fancy and want to be complemented for it. Make sure that your compliment isn't overdone, or they will see right through it. They are actually very conservative at heart.

Roosters are usually very attractive. They love the attention of others and are very sociable. Roosters are constantly on guard. They are skeptical of everything and are very hard to fool. Roosters should choose careers where their traits might give them an advantage. Roosters make good doctors, police detectives, and psychiatrist.

Rooster people never sit still. It is very out of character for them to be at home doing nothing. They get antsy when bored. It is wise for them to have multiple hobbies. If a Rooster gets bored, help them get up and moving. Find them something to do that will quench their thirst for busyness.

Roosters can do many things at once. They are great multi-taskers and they want everyone to know. Roosters may have more than a few jobs at once. They will find the time for each one. It's in their nature to overwork themselves. Another thing in their nature is to obsess over their physical appearance. Roosters can spend hours in front of the mirror trying to perfect their image.

In fact, they will spend vast amounts of money in order to *look good* to themselves and their peers. The Rooster can be a bargain hunter. They are always looking for a deal, but don't care too much about money. It's more for the excitement. The Rooster can be a dreamer. They tend to have their head in the clouds more than in reality. Help them to snap back to the present if they drift too far off.

The Rooster is still practical by nature. They are also resourceful and sharp with their decisions. They may talk big and get everyone around them excited for a dream they never actually fulfill. This can lead to many issues in their relationships. Roosters don't mean to lead people on. They really are sincere with their dreams, but they don't seem to achieve them as they promise they will. Be aware of this if you are entering a relationship with a Rooster.

One really good trait that Roosters possess is their unwavering loyalty. They make devoted friends and normally keep their promises. If only they can master this in regard to their dreams... Roosters make great partners. When they truly love someone, they will do anything and everything possible to make them happy.

Compatibility

The Rooster is most compatible with Snake, Ox, and Pig. They are least compatible with another Rooster, Rabbit, or the Goat.

12 THE DOG (YANG)

The Dog is one of the most lovable signs of The Chinese Zodiac. They are honest, faithful, and sincere. They usually hold traditional values and respect honor. The Dog will be the first to speak out against injustice of any kind.

They have many admirable traits and are respected by most of the people they know. They keep a small circle and are not very social animals. Dog people tend to keep to themselves and then slowly open up to the people around them. The Dog sign is very caring and compassionate. Dog people make good listeners and are quite intelligent. They are very modest and humble about their talents.

Dogs are very trustworthy. They are great at keeping secrets and dislike gossip. They are too good for such petty things. They try to distance themselves from people that are prone to it as well. Dog people make great companions. They can be a little mean when they are upset, but don't take it to heart. It is how they deal with anger. They may lash out, but none of it is from the heart.

At times, Dog people can be judgmental and defensive. This is usually only if something rubs them the wrong way. You can avoid this by doing and saying things that you know will make them happy. They will soon forget why they were upset and move on. There is no better companion than the dog.

The Dog would appear to have an old soul. They will take life too seriously while young and lighten up as they age. Dogs can be wise and make great teachers. Dog people are well rounded and do well in most careers. As long as they are happy and content with the work they are doing.

The Dog sign makes a good provider in a relationship. However, if they feel a lot of pressure against them, they might go a little crazy and overreact to things. In this case, they should talk things out with their partner. A lot of the time, the Dog attracts people that want and need to be taken care of. There is nothing wrong with that, as long as their partner is loving and caring of the Dog signs needs.

In love, Dog people are very generous, loving, and loyal. They are always honest and straightforward with their partner. Dog signs have a little trouble in the romantic department. This is due to their emotional instability and anxiety. Dogs need to calm down and be themselves. If they are in a mutually loving relationship, their partner will accept their quarks and learn to love them.

Dog signs are hard to dislike. They may come off a little weird and aloof at times, but they are quite the catch if you get to know them. Dog signs are great for marriage and the long-haul. If you are compatible with the Dog sign, it would be wise to pursue them. You won't be barking up the wrong tree!

Compatibility

The Dog is most compatible with Tiger, Horse, and Rabbit. They are least compatible with Dragon, Goat, and Ox.

13 THE PIG (YIN)

The Pig is the last sign of The Chinese Zodiac. If you are looking for the sincerest sign, then we have saved the best for last. Pigs are very sincere, pure, and tolerant people. They try to get along with everyone. They are honorable and caring, as well.

Pigs are very chivalrous and polite. They are also very reliable people. You can count on them if you ever need a favor. Pigs are very friendly and love to give. Most people prey on this and take advantage of the Pigs kind nature. Pig people are EXTREMLEY gullible. They are the most gullible sign of The Chinese Zodiac.

They tend to be aware of this, but justify by saying that they only see the *good* in people. That seems like a nice approach, but doesn't protect them at all. They should learn to be more guarded and skeptical like the Rooster. Pig people will sacrifice their happiness and well-being for others, time and time again.

The Pig makes a great companion. They are great friends and will always be there for you. Pigs aren't the first to strike up a conversation, but once you get them going, they'll never stop. Pigs have a great thirst for knowledge and are happy to share it at every opportunity they get. If you have a Pig friend, let them talk your ear off. It will make them happy that you listened.

Some Pig signs can come off a bit snobbish, but pay this no mind. They aren't stuck up at all. They are very well grounded in reality. People assume this about them because they care about their appearance and nice things. They just like to be presentable at all times. There is nothing more to it! Pigs tend to be stylish people. They like to flaunt their good taste. You should let them! There's no harm in it.

In a romantic relationship, Pigs can be very sensitive and sensual. They are also sweet and romantic in their own unique way. Pigs do great in marriage, but be warned, they can be possessive and jealous. Pigs are all around a great catch.

Compatibility

Pigs are most compatible with another Pig, Rabbit, or the Dragon. They are least compatible with Snake, Horse, and Dog.

14 LIFE

Life is an amazing learning experience that is never-ending. I hope that you have learned a lot about yourself and your peers from this simple guide. The next step is to apply what you have learned in to your everyday life. How do I do this? It's quite simple, really.

When possible, subtly or directly, figure out the zodiacs of the people around you. Use what you have learned from this guide to help you interact better with your peers and family. Feel free to keep this guide with you so you can easily reference it. I use The Chinese Zodiac in my daily life. I use it when making new friends, dating, and even financial decisions as well.

I have embraced The Chinese Zodiac for years. It's time for you to embrace it and be a better animal! This is a great starting point to repair your weaknesses and apply your strengths. Many individuals, businesses, and organizations swear by the teachings of The Chinese Zodiac. It's time for you to give it a shot and watch your social life change for the better.

I want to thank you for allowing me to share *The Chinese Zodiac: A Simple Guide* with you. I hope these teachings have helped you as much as they have helped me. Good luck on your journey in life, love, and success…

The Chinese Zodiac Personality Table

Animal	Personality characteristics	Year						
Rat	Imaginative, generous, successful, popular, curious	Feb 10, 1948 – Jan 28, 1949	Jan 28, 1960 – Feb 14, 1961	Feb 15, 1972 – Feb 2, 1973	Feb 2, 1984 – Feb 19, 1985	Feb 19, 1996 – Feb 6, 1997	Feb 7, 2008 – Jan 25, 2009	Jan 25, 2020 – Feb 11, 2021
Ox	Confident, honest, patient, conservative, strong	Jan 29, 1949 – Feb 16, 1950	Feb 15, 1961 – Feb 4, 1962	Feb 3, 1973 – Jan 22, 1974	Feb 20, 1985 – Feb 8, 1986	Feb 7, 1997 – Jan 27, 1998	Jan 26, 2009 – Feb 13, 2010	Feb 12, 2021 – Jan 31, 2022
Tiger	Sensitive, tolerant, brave, active, resilient	Feb 17, 1950 – Feb 5, 1951	Feb 5, 1962 – Jan 24, 1963	Jan 23, 1974 – Feb 10, 1975	Feb 9, 1986 – Jan 28, 1987	Jan 28, 1998 – Feb 15, 1999	Feb 14, 2010 – Feb 2, 2011	Feb 1, 2022 – Jan 21, 2023
Rabbit	Affectionate, kind, gentle, compassionate, merciful	Feb 6, 1951 – Jan 26, 1952	Jan 25, 1963 – Feb 2, 1964	Feb 11, 1975 – Jan 30, 1976	Jan 29, 1987 – Feb 16, 1988	Feb 16, 1999 – Feb 4, 2000	Feb 3, 2011 – Jan 22, 2012	Jan 22, 2023 – Feb 9, 2024
Dragon	Enthusiastic, intelligent, lively, energetic, innovative	Jan 27, 1952 – Feb 13, 1953	Feb 13, 1964 – Feb 1, 1965	Jan 31, 1976 – Feb 17, 1977	Feb 17, 1988 – Feb 5, 1989	Feb 5, 2000 – Jan 23, 2001	Jan 23, 2012 – Feb 9, 2013	Feb 10, 2024 – Feb 28, 2025
Snake	Charming, intuitive, romantic, highly perceptive, polite	Feb 14, 1953 – Feb 2, 1954	Feb 2, 1965 – Jan 20, 1966	Feb 18, 1977 – Feb 6, 1978	Feb 6, 1989 – Jan 26, 1990	Jan 24, 2001 – Feb 11, 2002	Feb 10, 2013 – Jan 30, 2014	Feb 29, 2025 – Feb 16, 2026
Horse	Diligent, friendly, sophisticated, talented, clever	Feb 3, 1954 – Jan 23, 1955	Jan 21, 1966 – Feb 8, 1967	Feb 7, 1978 – Jan 27, 1979	Jan 27, 1990 – Feb 14, 1991	Feb 12, 2002 – Jan 31, 2003	Jan 31, 2014 – Feb 18, 2015	Feb 17, 2026 – Feb 5, 2027
Sheep/ Goat	Artistic, calm, reserved, happy, kind	Jan 24, 1955 – Feb 11, 1956	Feb 9, 1967 – Jan 29, 1968	Jan 28, 1979 – Feb 15, 1980	Feb 15, 1991 – Feb 3, 1992	Feb 1, 2003 – Jan 21, 2004	Feb 19, 2015 – Feb 7, 2016	Feb 6, 2027 – Jan 25, 2028
Monkey	Witty, lively, flexible, humorous, curious	Feb 12, 1956 – Jan 30, 1957	Jan 30, 1968 – Feb 6, 1969	Feb 16, 1980 – Feb 4, 1981	Feb 4, 1992 – Feb 3, 1993	Jan 22, 2004 – Feb 8, 2005	Feb 8, 2016 – Feb 7, 2017	Jan 26, 2028 – Feb 12, 2029
Rooster	Shrewd, honest, communicative, motivated, punctual	Jan 31, 1957 – Feb 17, 1958	Feb 17, 1969 – Feb 5, 1970	Feb 5, 1981 – Jan 24, 1982	Jan 23, 1993 – Jan 22, 1994	Feb 9, 2005 – Jan 28, 2006	Jan 28, 2017 – Feb 15, 2018	Feb 13, 2029 – Feb 2, 2030
Dog	Loyal, honest, responsible, courageous, warm-hearted	Feb 18, 1958 – Feb 8, 1959	Feb 6, 1970 – Jan 26, 1971	Jan 25, 1982 – Feb 12, 1983	Feb 10, 1994 – Jan 30, 1995	Jan 29, 2006 – Feb 17, 2007	Feb 16, 2018 – Feb 4, 2019	Feb 3, 2030 – Jan 22, 2031
Pig	Sincere, tolerant, hard-working, honest, optimistic	Feb 8, 1959 – Jan 27, 1960	Jan 27, 1971 – Feb 4, 1972	Feb 13, 1983 – Feb 1, 1984	Jan 31, 1995 – Feb 18, 1996	Feb 18, 2007 – Feb 6, 2008	Feb 5, 2019 – Jan 24, 2020	Jan 23, 2031 – Feb 10, 2032

ABOUT THE AUTHOR

Aaron Howe is an author and Tiger sign from Los Angeles. That should explain it all. Thank you.